The Horten Ho 9
A Photo History

David Myhra

Schiffer Military History
Atglen, PA

Book Design by Ian Robertson.

Copyright © 1999 by David Myhra.
Library of Congress Catalog Number: 99-61379.

Printed in China.
ISBN: 0-7643-0916-1

We are interested in hearing from authors with book ideas on military topics.

Published by Schiffer Publishing Ltd.
4880 Lower Valley Road
Atglen, PA 19310 USA
Phone: (610) 593-1777
FAX: (610) 593-2002
E-mail: Schifferbk@aol.com.
Visit our web site at: www.schifferbooks.com
Please write for a free catalog.
This book may be purchased from the publisher.
Please include $3.95 postage.
Try your bookstore first.

In Europe, Schiffer books are distributed by:
Bushwood Books
6 Marksbury Road
Kew Gardens
Surrey TW9 4JF
England
Phone: 44 (0)181 392-8585
FAX: 44 (0)181 392-9876
E-mail: Bushwd@aol.com.

Try your bookstore first.

Beginnings of the Horten Ho 9

The *Horten* brothers', *Reimar* and *Walter*, most widely recognized powered aircraft design of the 1940s is their twin turbojet-powered all-wing fighter-bomber carrying the *RLM* designation *Ho 229*. Yet, the *Hortens* have their roots in motorless all-wing sailplanes, in fact, considered themselves primarily competition sailplane designers, constructors, and fliers. Yes and no. While teenagers they won their first aviation design award in July 1934 for the most innovative new sailplane design at the *Rhön Wasserkuppe* annual summer sailplane competitions. This sailplane was their wooden single- seat all-wing *Ho 1* and they won 600 *Reichsmarks* that summer. The *Hortens* constructed a new all- wing sailplane, the *Ho 2*, to be entered in the Rhön competitions of 1935. But it was not finished in time. It was modified to carry a 60 horsepower *Hirth M-60* engine with a pusher-type propeller. *Walter* enjoyed the opportunities and pleasures offered by powered flight. He especially liked aerobatics and could have been one of the best in the world if he had wanted to pursue this type of flying. *Reimar*, on the other hand, found the sailplane, its quietness and gentleness and maneuvering among the thermal currents more to his liking and temperament. Both volunteered for the *Luftwaffe*...*Walter* trained as a fighter pilot and *Reimar* went into transport gliders as a flight instructor. Later, in 1940 as a full-fledged *Bf 109* fighter pilot in the *Luftwaffe*, *Walter* was assigned administrative and personnel duties becoming the *Technical Officer* of *JG26* during their losing Battle for Britain he longed for a twin-engined all-wing fighter which he was calling his "German Mosquito." He did manage to score seven kills as *Adolf Galland's* wingman before all *Technical Officers* throughout the *Luftwaffe* were ordered never to fly combat. They were far too valuable in their leadership roles on the ground than to be lost in air-to-air combat. *Walter* found that scoring those seven kills

was a difficult job when put against the British "*Spitfire*" and he believed that it would be much easier for pilots with less flying than he had if they were flying a all-wing machine...a *Horten* all-wing machine. A twin-engine all-wing combat aircraft had initially been recommended to *Reimar* (1915-1994) and *Walter* (1913-1998) by their older brother *Wolfram* (1912-1940) who flew *He 111s* laying sea mines off the coast of France. Prior to his death in the crash of his *He 111, Wolfram* told his brothers of the pressing need for a *Horten* all-wing bomber, fighter, and reconnaissance machine in

order to fly non- stop around and over the British Isles. Later, *Walter* as a member of *JG26* had this point driven home as he watched his fellow *Luftwaffe* pilots lose their lives over England or crash in the English Channel after running out of gas attempting to return to their airfields in occupied France. Throughout their long career they would go on to design, construct, and fly over thirty different all-wing sailplane planforms and six motorized all-wing aircraft. This photo album concentrates on only one of their all-wing motorized aircraft...the prototype twin *Jumo 004B* turbojet-pow-

A trio of *Ho 229 V7* two-man day-fighters appearing waiting to take off clearance at a runway somewhere in Germany in search of high-flying American *B-29* "Super-fortress." Digital image by Mario Merino.

ered *Ho 9 V2*, its unintended sailplane version the *Ho 9 V1*, and the series production twin turbojet version under construction at war's end by *Gothaer Waggonfabrik AG "Gotha"* assigned the *RLM* designation *Ho 229*. *Reich Marshal Hermann Göring*, who had become quite supportive of the *Horten* all-wing awarded the two surviving brothers 500,000 *Reichmarks* for their design, construction, and first flight of the prototype *Ho 9*. *Göring* wanted a 3x1000 flying machine: 1,000 km/h [621 mph] speed, 1,000 kilogram [2,205 pounds] bomb load, and 1,000 kilometer [621 miles] range. The *Horten* brothers promised *Göring* these numbers courtesy of a *Horten* all-wing. *Göring* believed them without doubt while many of his advisors shook their heads in utter disbelief. But they were powerless to stop the *Horten* all-wing. Actually, it was the *Horten's* sailplane version which flew first...and unintended...in order to keep their promise to *Göring* because the *BMW 003* six stage compressor turbojet engines which were to power this

state-of-the-art machine were not ready for powered flight. They were abandoned and redesigned with a seven stage compressor. It was only then that the frame was converted into a sailplane while the *Horten's* constructed other frames to house *Jumo 004Bs*. *Göring's* money award was unique because both *Horten* brothers were members of *Göring's Luftwaffe* and in effect worked 24 hours a day for the *Reich Marshal* as did tens of thousands other men and woman so critics wondered why should they be paid extra? *Göring* did so because as *Reich Marshal* of the *Luftwaffe* he'd do what ever pleased him. The *Hortens*, too, strongly believed that they deserved the money...just as the money gifts *Lippisch*, *Messerschmitt*, and others received from *Göring* for their airplane designs from time to time. Nevertheless, the *Jumo 004B*-powered *Ho 9 V2* underwent flight testing between November 1944 and February 1945 at the Oranienburg airfield in the northwest suburbs of Berlin where the *Luftwaffe's* air reconnaissance

operations were located. Oranienburg was also where *Heinkel AG* built many of the single turbojet powered *He 162s* with POWs and inmates from the nearby Sacksenhausen *KZ*. The prototype *Ho 9 V2* crashed down upon returning to the airfield after high-speed test flying killing its test pilot *Erwin Ziller*. The cause of the accident is largely unknown.

This *Horten Ho 9* photo album is divided into three sections. The first section shows the evolution of the *Horten* engine-powered all-wing machines. The *Ho 2A* sailplane was modified to a powered machine and called the *Ho 2B*. This machine would be later modified again to carry out research on the aerodynamic correctness of placing round air intakes in the center section's leading edge for the *Ho 9 V2*. It's center section was modified again into a double sweep back to test the aerodynamics of the proposed two man *Ho 229 V7* day fighter/night fighter. However the majority of this first section chronicles the rise of the twin-engine *Horten* all-wing flying machine beginning with the *Ho 5A*, *5B*, and *5C* and the *Ho 7A*. *Reimar* had considered using their *Ho 7* as a test bed for several engine combinations such as using the *Daimler-Benz DB 601E* of 1,375 horsepower which were powering the *Bf 109E* at the time. In addition, *Reimar* had given thought to mounting one or two *Argus As 014* 660 pound [300 kilogram] thrust pulse jet engines between the *Ho 7's* twin *Argus As 10C* 240 horsepower piston engines. He didn't, of course and gifted digital image artist *Mario Merino* has created images of *Reimar's* daydreaming regarding the placing of additional engines the *Ho 7A*. About this same time *Walter* learned of the extensive research into a piston-less aeroengine. This was the axial flow turbojet engine under development by *BMW*, *Bramo*, *Junkers Jumo*, and *Heinkel-Hirth*. *BMW* had purchased *Bramo* and *Dr.-Ing. Hermann Oestrich* told *Walter* (who had been transferred to the *Jagdfluginspektion* [Inspection of Fighters-Berlin] at the request of *General von Döring*.

Reimar Horten (left) and *Walter Horten* (right) with *Horten Flugzeug's* capable test pilot *Heinz Schiedhauer's* white pet dog "*Purzel*," or "elf." About 1944.

Von Döring knew Walter Horten well because earlier he had been one of the founding fathers/leaders of JG26 and Walter was a member of the administrative staff) about Bramo works small diameter axial flow engine. It appeared that two of these small diameter turbojets would fit nicely within the center section of a Ho 7-sized all-wing. Reimar dropped all his ideas regarding the use of the DB 601E and the As 014 pulse jets and began designing an all-wing fighter powered by twin Bramo small diameter turbojet engines. Mario Merino has provided digital illustrations on how the Bramo-powered Ho 7 might have looked. The Bramo turbojet was abandoned by BMW in favor of a more powerful axial design known as the 003. This six-stage compressor 003 engine was running but its thrust output did not reach anticipated design projections. The six-stage compressor 003 was abandoned in favor of a seven stage compressor 003A.

The second section features the design, construction, and flight testing of the Ho 9 V1 sailplane and the twin turbojet powered Ho 9 V2. The Ho 9 was found to experience a side-to-side oscillation during flight and known as a "Dutch Walk." Not a very good characteristic for a proposed high-speed fighter machine. Walter felt that something had to be done to correct it. Reimar felt that a good pilot could learn to live with the 9 second side-to-side oscillations. Walter believed this condition could be effectively corrected through the use of a vertical fin with an attached rudder. Mario Merino has created several digital images showing how the Ho 9 V2 might have looked with a vertical fin/rudder. Finally, the reader is shown digital images of the Ho 9 V2's crash site at Oranienburg airfield on 18

February 1945. This crash site has been reconstructed from eye witness accounts.

The third and final section in this photo album features the Ho 229 V3 under serial production by Gothaer Waggonfabrik AG "Gotha" at war's end. No V3's were yet flight ready when the war in Europe ended on 9 May 1945 but two of the machines were close to be complete when the American Army found the abandoned Gotha workshops where the Ho 229 V3, V4, and possibly the V5 and V6 were being constructed. The V3 and V4 were gathered up by General George McDonald head of American Army Air Force Intelligence-Europe and placed in a captured Luftwaffe aircraft holding site. The British asked for and received the V3 from McDonald. It was transported to RAE-Farnborough where it was evaluated with the idea in mind to remove the twin Jumo 004Bs and replace them with Rolls-Royce centrifugal "Nene" turbojet engines. It appeared that the larger diameter of the "Nene" would spoil the aerodynamics of the all-wing and the idea was abandoned. RAE-Farnborough shipped the Ho 229 V3 to Freeman Field, Ohio about October 1945. No information is currently available to this au-

thor regarding the fate of the uncompleted Ho 229 V4 and it was probably scrapped along with the bare center section frames of the V5 and V6. General McDonald was not a fan of the all-wing planform and found no good reason to bring the Horten all-wings to the USA. Mario Merino has provided digital images of the Ho 229 including the V3, the V3 with a vertical fin/rudder, and the two-man day fighter and night fighter V7.

Readers wishing biographical information on the life and work of the Horten brothers are encouraged to read the author's "The Horten Brothers and Their All-Wing Aircraft" published by Schiffer Publishing 1997. Additional information regrading Ho 9 and proposed variations such as the Ho 9B, Ho 9C, as well as the Ho 18B "Amerika Bomber" project can be found in the author's "Secret Aircraft Designs of the Third Reich" published also by Schiffer Publishing 1998.

David Myhra
March 1999
Ft. Myers, Florida

The teenage Horten brothers, Reimar (left) and Walter (right), standing by their award winning Ho 1 sailplane in the grass at the Bonn Hangelar airfield about Spring 1934. Walter is wearing a parachute harness and has just finishing making a flight with the wood-built all-wing. Ten years later the two brothers will have built and test flown a twin turbojet powered all-wing...their Ho 9 V2. Absolutely amazing even more so with only 100 plus workers compared to the tens of thousands employed by the four aircraft companies in Germany to put jet-powered aircraft into the air: Arado [Ar 234B/C], Messerschmitt [Me 262], Heinkel [He 162] and Junkers [Me 263 and the pieced together Ju 287 V1].

Reimar Horten at the Horten ranch, Argentina about Fall 1982. Photograph by the author.

The brand new Ho 2A sailplane with its outer wings yet to be covered shown inside a hangar at the Bonn Hangelar, 1935. The Hortens had hoped to enter their second sailplane in the Rhön Wasserkuppe Summer sailplane competitions but it was not ready when the registration deadline arrived. The Ho 2A sailplane had a wingspan of 54.1 feet [16.5 meters].

The *Ho 2A* shown outside the Bonn *Hangelar* prior to its maiden flight. About May 1935. The *Ho 1's* outer wings could not be removed. In the *Ho 2A* the *Hortens* made the outer wings easily detachable thus very portable. All *Horten* flying machines, both powered and sail were built from this time on with detachable outer wings including the twin turbojet powered *Ho 9 V2.*

Although the *Hortens* stated that they were sailplane enthusiasts, they wasted no time in designing and constructing a motor-powered all-wing...the *Ho 2B (*sometimes referred to as the *Ho 2M...M* for motor). It was their *Ho 2A* modified to carrying a single *Hirth* 60 horsepower air-cooled engine with a pusher propeller. About October 1935.

In the foreground is the *Ho 2B.* In the background is the *Horten* brothers 1st twin engined all-wing...the brand new yet to be flown, the all plastic *Ho 5A.* The *Ho 5A* was powered by twin *Hirth* 60 horsepower air-cooled engines. Troisdorf about May 1937.

The *Ho 5A* had dual seats yet the cockpit area was completely smooth. The *Ho 5A*'s dark appearance came from the plastic material produced by *Dynamit-Noble AG* called "*Dynal.*" This prototype aircraft covering was extremely difficult to work. Performance figures are not available because the *Ho 5A* crashed and was destroyed during lift off on its maiden flight. The crash was due to a miscalculation of the center of gravity by *Reimar.* Both *Hortens* were inside the machine when it crashed but escaped serious injury. It would be the last time both brothers would be together in one of their designs during its maiden flight.

The plastic composition *Ho 5A* shown here at Troisdorf Spring 1937 featuring its twin hand-carved wooden propellers attached to *Hirth* 60 horsepower air-cooled engines. The nose wheel retracted, however, the main gear was fixed.

The remains of the *Ho 5A* after crashing on its maiden flight June 1937 due to *Reimar's* miscalculation of the aircraft's center of gravity. Amazingly neither *Walter* or *Reimar* were seriously hurt.

A close-up view of the broken wooden propellers on the ill-fated *Ho 5A* after crashing on its maiden flight. *Dynamit-Noble AG* had invested 40,000 *Reichsmarks* in the *Ho 5A*.

The *Horten* brother's second twin piston engine all-wing prototype...the *Ho 5B*. This machine was constructed out of conventional material such as wood. It differed from the *Ho 5A* in that the *5B's* dual seats had their own individual raised cockpits.

A ground-level view of the *Ho 5B. Reimar Horten* stated that the *5B* was capable of 311 mph [500 km/h] forward speed. *Reimar* sought to interest the *RLM's Gottfried Reidenbach* in the machine but he was bent on putting the *Junkers Ju 88* into serial production. *Reidenbach*, a highly insecure and generally mean-spirited individual, in effect told *Reimar* that he knew nothing about aircraft design and so get lost. The *Ju 88's* top speed was about 248 mph [397 km/h] and its losses during the *Luftwaffe's* Battle for Britain was staggering...a design failure as a high-speed fighter/bomber.

A close up view of the *Ho 5Bs* clean plastic leading edge panels installed in the center section. These panels appear tinted in this photo but they were clear and allowed the pilot a complete view of the runway when landing.

A view of the *Ho 5B's* center section from its trailing edge between its twin piston engines looking forward to the twin pilot cockpit canopies. The center section's surface is covered with sheet plywood. The *Ho 5B* was put into storage in September 1938 for a lack of interest by the *RLM*...actually a total rejection.

The first *Horten* powered all-wing designed with a military application in mind...the former twin seat *Ho 5B* reconditioned by *Peschke Flugzeugbau Werke*-Minden as the single seat *Ho 5C*. Shown in flight in this photograph. Göttingen airfield about 1942.

The single-seat *Ho 5C* in banking turn. It had been left outdoors since 1939 after losing its indoor storage. The machine seriously deteriorated and was reborn again as a single-seater by *Peschke Flugzeugbau Werke*-Minden in 1942 after about 1,000 hours of work.

A port side nose view of the only *Ho 5C* constructed...the *Peschke Flugzeug Werke*- modified *Ho 5B*. During the repair *Peschke* removed the plywood covering from the old *Ho 5B* and replaced it with aluminum. The *5C* was later written off in the Spring of 1943 after *Professor Dr.-Ing. Josef Stüper* from *AVA-Göttingen* hit a hangar's roof during a abortive takeoff. The pilot professor was not seriously injured but the *Ho 5C* was never repaired.

A poor quality photo of the *Ho 5C* as seen from its port rear side. *Walter Horten* is standing on a ladder placed in front of the machine. The *5C's* flight controls on the port outer wing are nicely seen in this photograph. *Walter* wanted a larger flying machine...a back to back two seater with the rear seat occupied by a gunner. Göttingen about 1942.

The Horten Ho 9 V1 & V2

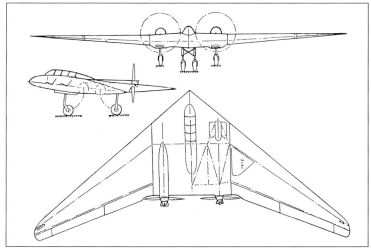

Pen and ink three-view general outline drawing of the *Ho 7*.

How the *Ho 7* might have looked with the addition of a single *BMW 003* turbojet engine placed between its twin *Argus As 10-C3*s if *Walter* had had his way. In addition to the single *003* there were plans to install twin turbojets in an over and under arrangement. Digital image by *Mario Merino*.

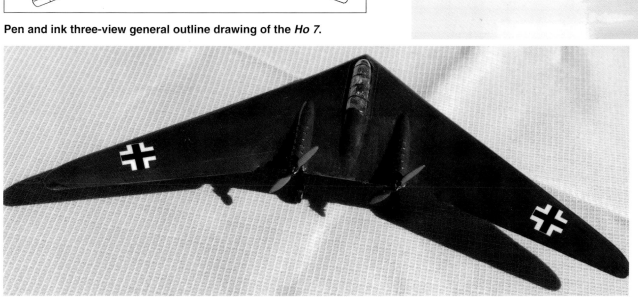

An overhead view of the *Ho 7* painted in green camouflage. Scale model by *Reinhard Roeser*.

A stunning view of the *Ho 7* as it passes overhead.

A head-on view of the new *Ho 7* at Göttingen.

The *Ho 7* flying out front and off to starboard and presenting a very, very small cross section signature to enemy radar.

The *Ho 7* as seen from its rear starboard side. The sheet metal covering the drive shafts have been removed for maintenance. It's *Argus As 10 C3's* are buried entirely within the wing.

Below: *Reimar Horten's* idea to improve the performance of the *Ho 7* as a military machine by adding a single *Argus As 014* pulse jet. The pulse jet would have been mounted between the two *As* piston engines. Digital image by *Mario Merino*.

The *Ho 7* with its drive shafts covers in place, secured, and the machine is ready for flight.

A rear-starboard view of the *Ho 7* modified with the addition of a single *Argus As 014* pulse jet on the upper surface of the center section. Digital image by *Mario Merino*.

The same *Ho 7*, however, with twin *Argus As 014* pulse jets mounted on the light blue underside of the *Ho 7* to augment its twin piston engines. Digital image by *Mario Merino*.

The *Ho 7* seen here with its twin *Argus As 014* pulse jets burning at their full thrust of 660 pounds [300 kilograms] each.

A full starboard side view of the proposed *Ho 7* powered by twin *DB 601-E* piston engines. Digital image by *Mario Merino*.

Reimar Horten considered another engine alterative in order to obtain additional performance from the *Ho 7* and that was to substitute the twin 8-cylinder *Argus As 10-C3* piston engines of 240 horsepower (270 hp at takeoff) each for twin 12-cylinder *Daimler-Benz DB 601-E* piston engines of 1,375 horsepower each. This was the engine used in the *Bf 109E* and the *Ho 7's* performance would have been nothing short of awesome. Digital image by *Mario Merino*.

A nose starboard side view of the proposed *DB 601-E* powered *Ho 7*. Digital image by *Mario Merino*.

A close-up view of the *Ho 7* with a pair of 1,375 horsepower *DB 601-E* piston engines. One of the these powered the *Bf 109.* A flight ready *Ho 7* weighed 4,409 pounds [2,000 kilograms]. Each *As 10-C3* engine weighed 475 pounds [215 kilograms], produced 240 horsepower and giving about 0.5 horsepower per pound. On the other hand each *DB 601-E* engine weighed 1,400 pounds [635 kilograms] and produced almost 1.0 horsepower per pound of weight. Thus, two *DB 601-E*s would provide about 2,750 horsepower verse 480 horsepower from two *As 10-C3* engines. The *Ho 7* would weigh an additional 1,850 pounds or about 6,259 pounds flight ready with a pair of *DB 601-E*s. Nevertheless, the *Ho 7* would have 0.44 horsepower per pound with the *DB 601-E* verse 0.11 horsepower per pound with a pair of *As 10-C3.* The re-engined *Ho 7* would have really screamed with a pair of DB *601-E*s. Too bad it was never tried. Digital image by *Mario Merino.*

A starboard side view of a *Ho 7* with a pair of *BMW 003* six-stage compressor turbojet engines mounted on the center section...one on the upper surface and one on the lower surface. Digital image by *Mario Merino.*

Above: The small diameter axial turbojet engine of *BMW/Bramo [3302]* which *Dr.-Ing. Hermann Oestrich* wanted the *Horten* brothers to consider using in their project *Ho 9.*

Left: A *Ho 7* above and off to starboard showing its awesome propulsion system: a pair of *BMW 003s* mounted over and under the center section plus a pair of *As 10-C3* piston engines on the upper center section surface. Digital image by *Mario Merino*.

Below: The initial *Ho 9* turbojet powered (concept #1) design and powered by a pair of *BMW/Bramo* [3302] diameter axial-flow turbojet engines. This *Ho 9* abandoned after *BMW* abandoned the *3302* jet engine program. Digital image by *Mario Merino*.

The proposed *Ho 9* powered by twin *BMW/Brano* [*3302*] small diameter axial turbojet engines. Digital image by *Mario Merino*.

Reimar had decided not to modify the *Ho 7* with the addition of larger horsepower piston engines, pulse jets, and so on. He felt the *Ho 7's* structure was not strong enough so he was thinking of an entirely new stronger machine along the same general lines as the *Ho 7* which he was calling the *Ho 9*. Scale model by the *Horten Flugzeugbau*. About 1942.

A starboard nose view of the initial *Ho 9's* center section frame with a small diameter *BMW/Brano* [*3302*] axial turbojet engine installed. This initial version of the *Ho 9* was abandoned after *Dr.-Ing. Oestrich* told the *Horten* brothers that *BMW* was abandoning the small diameter turbojet engine in favor of a more powerful six-stage compressor axial-flow turbojet called the *003*.

A full starboard side view of the initial *Ho 9* design featuring its two man tandem seating cockpit arrangement. Digital image by *Mario Merino*.

Left: A head on view of the initial *Ho 9* design powered by twin small diameter *BMW/ Brano* turbojet engines. Air intake for the turbines were to be located in the center section's leading edge. In this photograph of the scale model, the *Ho 9* is shown carrying two 1,102 pound [*500* kilogram] *SC* bombs.

A rear port side view of the initial *Ho 9* design. Its two man tandem greenhouse style cockpit canopy is nicely shown in this photo of the scale model.

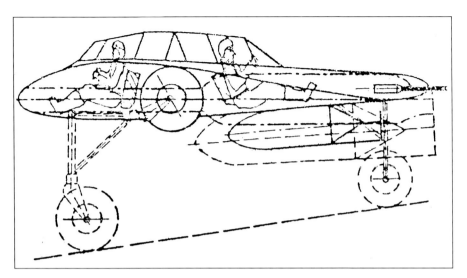

A pen and ink drawing of the initial *Ho 9* concept and showing the seating position of its two man crew. The rear sitting crew man operated the machine gun placed aft in the trailing edge of the center section. It appears that the nose wheel retracted up into the center section in the space between the pilot and gunner. The *Ho 9* is shown carrying an externally mounted bomb.

Two, two man crew *Ho 9's* on defensive maneuvers over Germany. Digital image by *Mario Merino*.

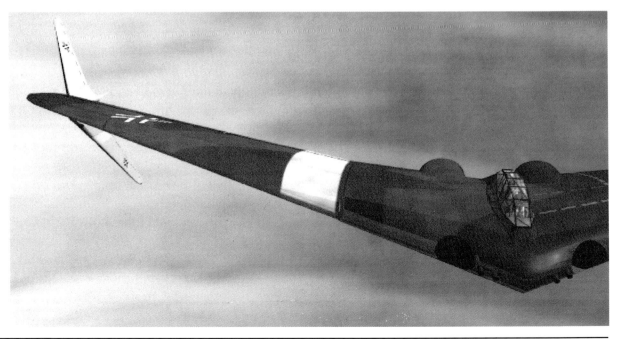

A two man *Ho 9* featuring its starboard wing while a second *Ho 9* appears in a banking turn off its starboard wing tip. Digital image by *Mario Merino*.

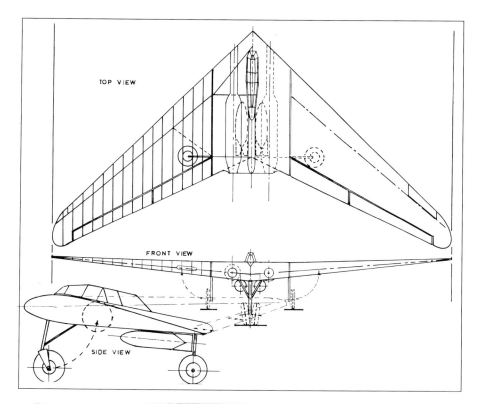

TOP VIEW

FRONT VIEW

SIDE VIEW

Above: The 2nd concept *Ho 9* was designed with a pointed center section trailing edge. Here are a pair of 2nd concept *Ho 9s* in flight each powered by a pair of *BMW 003* six-stage compressor turbojet engines. Unfortunately for the *Horten* brothers, the six-stage compressor engine was abandoned by *BMW*. Instead of throwing the center section frame away, the Hortens turned it into a motorless sailplane and called it the *Ho 9 V1*. Digital image by *Mario Merino*.

Above Left: A pen and ink three-view general arrangement drawing of the initial *Ho 9* concept with its green house-style cockpit and powered containing twin small diameter *BMW/Bramo 3302* turbojet engines.

Left: *Horten Flugzeugbau* artist's vision of the 2nd *Ho 9* concept turbojet-powered all-wing fighter. The *Horten's* have eliminated the gunner from the cockpit and as a result are able to make it more streamlined. The pilot himself operates the twin cannon mounted in the nose of the center section.

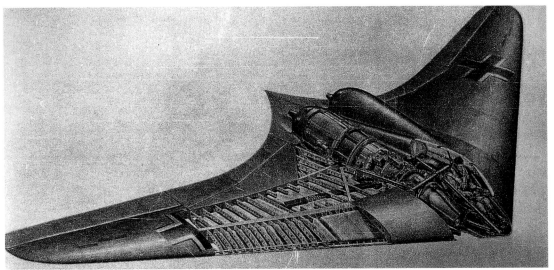

In this see-through illustration of the 2ⁿᵈ *Ho 9* concept, the *Horten's* are continuing to power their fighter with *BMW* axial-flow turbojets. These turbines were to be the six-stage compressor *003* models. However, the six-stage, like the small diameter turbines [*3302*] underdevelopment from *Bramo* before *BMW* bought them out, were abandoned. *BMW* found the six-stage compressor *003* not powerful enough and had to redesign the engine around a seven-stage compressor. This *Ho 9* could have been up and running by 1943 had the engines been ready. However, even *Junkers Jumo* was having problems with their *004B*, too, as we have seen from the history of the *Me 262's* prolonged development.

The *Horten Flugzeugbau* workshop where the *Ho 9's* construction was started. Four or more center section frames had to be designed, built, modified and in a couple of cases abandoned and started over as turbojet engine diameters grew larger. The buildings survived WWII and look pretty much the same today.

Behind these large doors which admitted 1 1/2 ton trucks for maintenance is where the *Horten* brothers and their faithful workers laboring two shifts per day, seven days a week in order to get their turbojet-powered all-wing *Ho 9* into the air as *Reich Marshal Göring* had been promised.

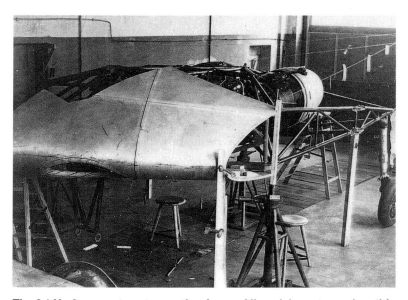

The 2nd *Ho 9* concept center section frame. All work has stopped on this machine because the *Hortens* have been told that the six-stage compressor *BMW 003* which *Dr.-Ing. Oestrich* had promised them has been abandoned in favor of a seven-stage compressor *003*. Air intakes for the initial *003* were located on the under side of the center section's leading edge.

The port side air intake metal wire frame is featured in this photo of the 2nd *Ho 9* concept center section frame. The wire frame is just to check the fit of the aluminum tube which was being crafted as the air intake duct.

A view of the aft area of the Ho 9 2nd concept center section frame. A empty BMW six-stage compressor *003* starboard turbine lifts high out over near the *Ho 9's* trailing edge. It had been installed to check for fit and alignment as they waited for the ready-run to engine.

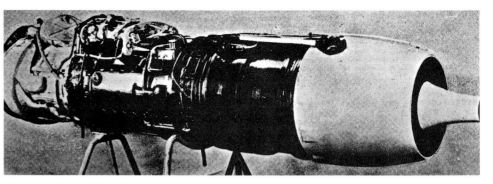

The *BMW 003A* seven-stage compressor turbojet unit. The *Horten* brothers never did receive this turbine for the *Ho 9* even the *Ho 229*. The limited production made these units somewhat rare and about 75% of them were given over to powering the *Arado Ar 234B* with the remaining units placed in the *Heinkel He 162* single engine "people's fighter."

The starboard wing root side of the 2ⁿᵈ *Ho 9* concept center section frame. It appears that this center section was being built more compactly with everything seemingly crowded together.

The *BMW 003A* separated into its four general component sections. Left to right: thrust nozzle assembly, combustion chamber with turbine "hot wheel," seven-stage compressor, and air intake duct.

With the cancellation of the six-stage compressor *BMW 003*, the center section frame was suddenly useless. The *Horten's* removed the empty *003* units and began placing plywood covering over the center section converting it into a engineless sailplane. Here *Horten* workers are making the necessary modifications directed by *Reimar*.

A view of the *Ho 9 V1* as seen from its starboard side. Originally fuel for the twin turbines would have been carried in metal tanks in the outer wings. No fuel tanks were placed in the *V1's* wings.

A pen and ink line drawing of the 2nd *Ho 9* concept flying machine. The engineless center section is narrower than that of the *Ho 9 V2* and the *V3*.

Left: A view of the *Ho 9 V1's* starboard wing and wing control surfaces. A dozen men could carry one of the outer wings. The dark vertical lines is putty filing up and smoothing over joints in the plywood covering.

Bottom Left: Two *Horten* workers are installing the *Ho 9 V1's* cockpit windscreen's metal frame prior to covering over the nose portion of the center section. In the foreground is the port outer wing.

Bottom Right: The *Ho 9 V1* center section looking very complete except for the cockpit canopy. The open box at the trailing edge is where the drag parachute was stored during flight. During flight it was covered by a light-weight two-piece door. The parachute upon release exited out and above the trailing edge.

A starboard side view of the *Ho 9 V1's* center section and only a matter of a few weeks away from being flight ready. It appears that some additional work needs to be done on the cockpit canopy's rear portion but otherwise the center section frame appears complete.

The *Ho 9 V1* being towed to the starting line by truck where it will be connected by cable to the *Horten's He 111* tow aircraft. This was the *Ho 9 V1's* maiden flight and flown by test pilot *Heinz Scheidhauer*. Göttingen, 28 February 1944.

A rear port side view of the *Ho 9 V1* under tow on a snowy day from its Göttingen hangar on 28 February 1944 to the active runway for its maiden flight.

A rear starboard side view of the *Ho 9 V1*. The new sailplane is about to be disconnected from its tow truck and attached to one end of a cable. The other end is attached to a *He 111 Horten Flugzeugbau* tow aircraft. The flight itself was satisfying, however when *Heinz Scheidhauer* landed he put the *V1* down on the runway about mid way and it just kept going and going. In order to slow the *V1* down *Scheidhauer* had to retract the nose wheel.

The *Ho 9 V1* nose down on the snow-covered runway at Göttingen airfield. *Scheidhauer* needed to do this in order to slow the *V1* down otherwise he might have hit the hangars at the end of the landing strip. The *V1* suffered only minor damage. *Scheidhauer* was unhurt except possibly his ego a little.

Horten test pilot *Heinz Scheidhauer* photographed at Göttingen in May 1943. *Scheidhauer* is leaning up against the wing of a *Ho 4A* sailplane.

A rear port side view of the *Ho 9 V1* photographed at Göttingen airfield Spring 1944.

A nose on view of the *Ho 9 V1* photographed at Göttingen airfield Spring 1944.

The *Ho 9 V1* rear view photographed at Göttingen airfield Spring 1944. The *Ho 9's* drag parachute can be seen directly aft the cockpit canopy.

A front starboard view of the *Ho 9 V1* photographed at Göttingen airfield Spring 1944.

Bottom Left: The cockpit of the *Ho 9 V1* sailplane. Instruments include: nose wheel indicator top; below left to right...speed indicator, turn and bank (blind flying) indicator, compass, climb and descent indicator, and altitude. The small square silver colored box to the right of the instrument panel is the electric master switch.

Bottom Right: A German flight suit manufacturer testing their prototype pressure suit in the *Ho 9 V1* Spring 1944. The *V1's* cockpit was too small for an effective test because when the suit was inflated the pilot inside couldn't move much even turn his head. Testing was abandoned.

Walter Horten describing the tow line attachment mechanism used on the *Ho 9 V1* sailplane to fellow officers from the *RLM*. Spring 1944.

Horten workers hand pushing the *Ho 9 V1* into its hangar at Göttingen. Taken from the roof of the *V1's* hangar. Spring 1944.

Horten workers are towing the *Ho 9 V1* out to the runway where it will be flight tested. *Reimar* never flew the *V1*, however, *Walter* flew the sailplane often. Göttingen airfield. Spring 1944.

The *Ho 9 V1* in a final landing approach at the Göttingen airfield with *Heinz Scheidhauer* at the controls. Spring 1944.

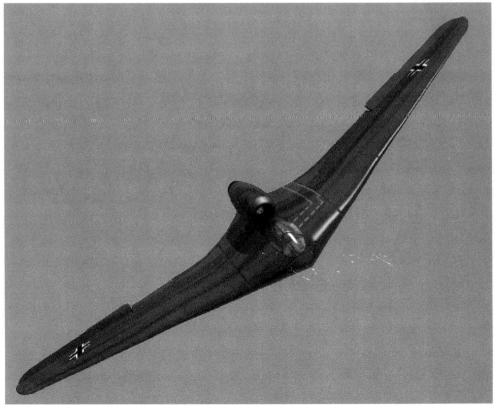

Walter Horten had thought of placing a single *Jumo 004B* turbojet on the upper surface of the *Ho 9 V1* behind the cockpit canopy in order to obtain flight test data on jet-powered flight. The *Ho 9 V2* with its twin *Jumo 004Bs* would not be ready for flight testing until November 1944 and *Walter* was getting nervous waiting as American fighter escorts were swarming all over German skies. Flight testing the *V2* might not happen due to the American dominance of the skies. Then, too, the war might be over before the *V2* was flight ready. Digital image by *Mario Merino*.

The *Ho 9 V1* with a single *Jumo 004B*. It is not entirely clear why *Reimar* did not place a single *Jumo 004B* on the *V1* but it didn't happen probably because *Reimar* was putting all his energies into making the *9 V2* flight ready given all his delays due to the numerous engine changes and the center section frame modifications required. Digital image by *Mario Merino*.

Bottom Right: An American Army soldier ponders the unusual-looking *Ho 9 V1* at Brandis/Leipzig airfield.

The *Ho 9 V1* found by General McDonald's Army Air Force Intelligence team at Brandis/Leipzig airfield early May 1945. Its outer wings have been removed and placed on sawhorses, however, the entire sailplane appears to be in good condition now at war's end. General McDonald's men took the *V1* to a *Luftwaffe* collection center near Mersesberg for evaluation.

The final end of the *Ho 9 V1...sitting* on the grass prior to its destruction with its cockpit canopy plexiglass smashed out. One of the *V1's* outer wings appears in the background in the photograph's upper left hand corner.

It is well documented that the single seat *Ho 9 V2* was powered by a pair of *Jumo 004Bs* when it under went its flight testing January/February 1945 at Oranienburg. Even after the *RLM* promised the *Hortens* a pair of *004Bs* for the *V2*, they later asked the *Hortens* to wait and install a pair of *BMW 003A* seven-stage compressor turbojet engines. "What, modify *V2's* center section frame again?" Shown is the *Ho 9 V2* in flight powered by a pair of *BMW 003A* turbojet engines. Digital image by *Mario Merino*.

Horten Flugzeugbau graphic artist *Richard Keller's* rendition of the *Jumo 004B*-powered *Ho 9 V2*. The way he pictured the *V2* with its twin turbojet engines buried deep within the center section is pretty much the way the *V2* turned out when it was finally flight ready in December 1944. Göttingen early 1944.

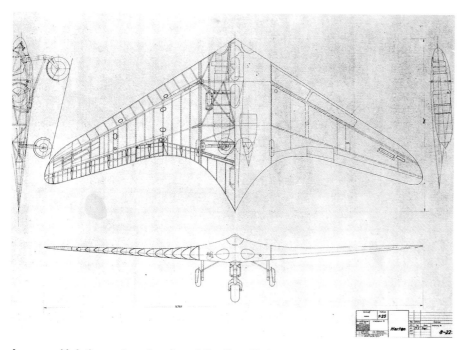

Roll out day of the *Ho 9 V2's* center section frame welded up to carry twin *Jumo 004Bs*. Finally! This center section had been modified so many times due to turbo-jet engines promised then denied that *Reimar* feared its strength had been compromised so the *V2* should not be flown at top speed or through wild maneuvers such as rolls, high speed dives, and so on.

A pen and ink three-view drawing of the *Ho 9 V2* from WWII. This one appears pretty accurate in terms of where *Reimar* placed the Jumo *004B* turbojet engines in the center section and this is why it is included in this collection of photographs on the *Ho 9*. It is not so accurate in terms of the nose wheel in fact the draftsman appears to have taken the type of nose wheel used on the *Ho 229 V3*. *Reimar* used the *He 177's* tail wheel for the nose wheel assembly on his *Ho 9 V2*.

The starboard side of the *Ho 9 V2's* bare center section frame. Its huge nose wheel, a former *He 177* tail wheel, dominates the frame. The two main wheels came from a *Bf 109* fighter. The rectangle bar seen at the nose (cockpit area) of the *V2* is where instruments for the twin *004Bs* would be located.

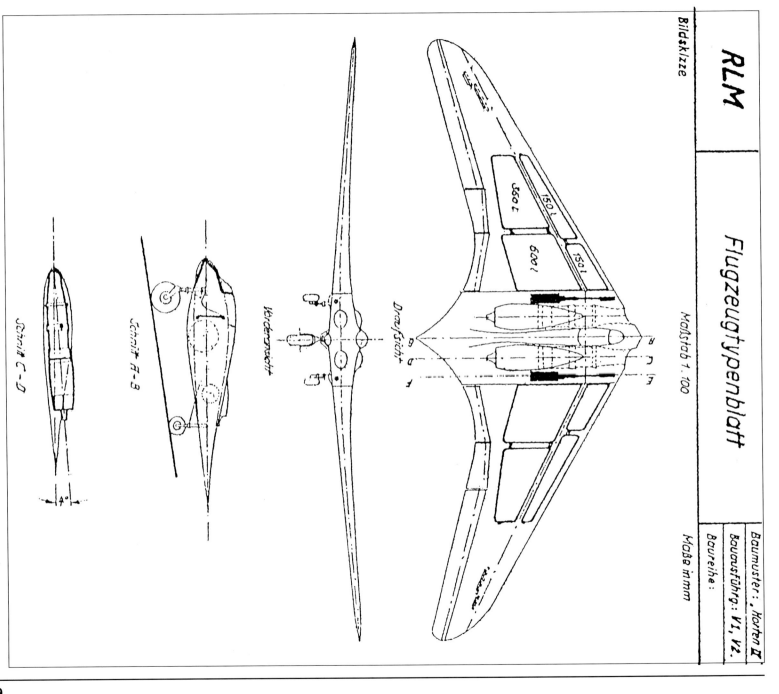

RLM

Bildskizze

Flugzeugtypenblatt

Maßstab 1:100

Maße in mm

Baumuster: „Horten Ⅸ
Bauausführg: VI, V2.
Baureihe:

Schnitt C-D

Schnitt A-B

Vorderansicht

Draufsicht

A copy of an original pen and ink three-view line drawing of the *Ho 9 V2*. In order to get the super smooth upper surface *Reimar* pushed the *004Bs* so far aft that the *V2* required 1,764 pounds [800 kilograms] of lead ballast spread around the nose area of the center section.

A see-through illustration of the *Ho 9 V2* as seen from its port side. Digital image by *Mario Merino*.

A transparent close up of the *Ho 9 V2's* center section, cockpit, and *Jumo 004Bs*. Digital image by *Mario Merino*.

A transparent view of the *Ho 9 V2* shortly after take off with its landing gear still down. Digital image by *Mario Merino*.

A close up of the *Ho 9 V2's* trailing edge center section. The starboard side main gear taken from a *Bf 109* is clearly shown.

The *Ho 9 V2* with its outer wings attached. The center section covering has not yet been attached, perhaps as work continues on its twin *Jumo 004Bs* which dominate the center section's trailing edge. Both of its starboard wing tip rudders (upper and lower) are extended. Gottingen about Fall 1944.

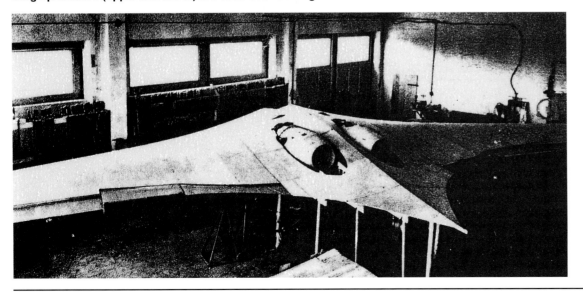

An overhead view of the *Ho* 9 *V2* appearing all covered over with sheet plywood. Notice how clean the *Horten* workshop is kept at all times?

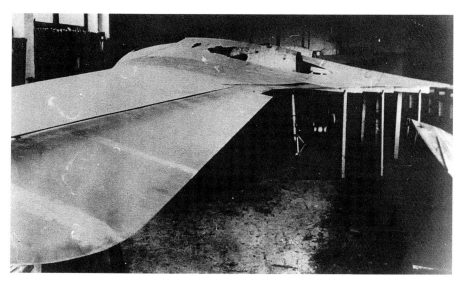

An eye-level view of the *Ho 9 V2* from its port side and featuring its port wing control surfaces. Metal (tin) covering around the exposed portions of the *Jumo 004Bs* have yet to be fitted.

The starboard side *9 V2* upper and lower wing tip rudders fully extended. When *Gotha* was getting the *Ho 229* ready for serial production they eliminated the lower wing tip rudders indicating, it appears, that *Gotha* was thinking of the *Ho 229* not as a fighter with a need for a large amount of turning (rudder surface) ability but as a bomber which flew straight mile after mile?

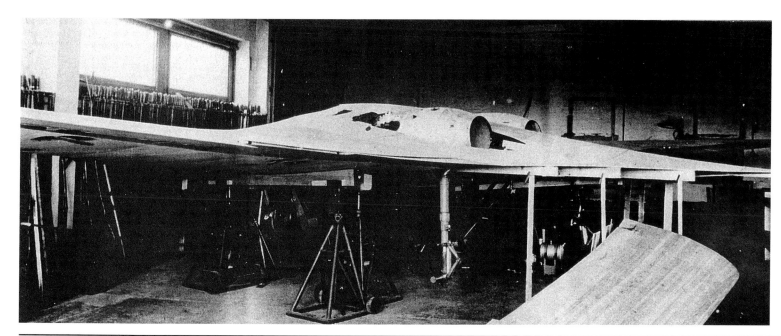

Another eye-level view of the *Ho 9 V2* in its workshop near Göttingen. About Fall 1944.

The starboard side upper surface wing tip rudders partially extended as seen on the *Ho 9 V1.*

A close up view of starboard side full open upper wing tip rudders on the *Ho 9 V2.* Notice that the wing surface has yet to be covered over with joint putty.

The port side upper surface wing tip rudders almost fully closed as seen on the *Ho 9 V1.*

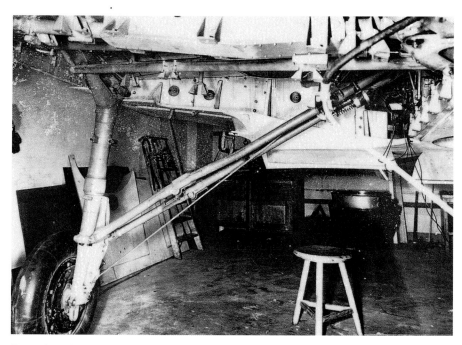

Port wing side main landing wheel/gear on the new *Ho 9 V2.* To the right in the photo can be seen the fully extended center section-mounted drag rudder located just above the wooden three-legged stool.

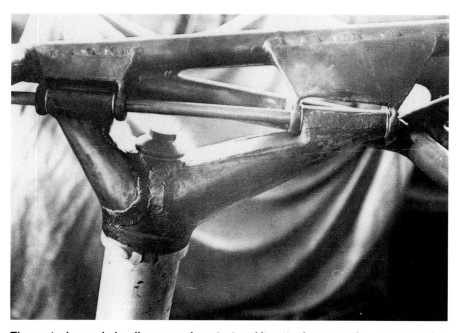

The port wing main landing gear oleo-strut and its attachment to the center section frame. All this looks pretty fragile and indeed, once when test pilot *Erwin Ziller* came in at Oranienburg for a hard landing, the trailing edge where the oleo struts were attached were deflected up ward almost 3/4 of an inch and representing major damage...more like a crash because the *9 V2* could not be flown until the damage was repaired.

The port side of the *Ho 9 V2* featuring its main landing gear from *Bf 109's.*

A close up of the *Bf 109* main landing gear on the port side of *Ho 9 V2* under construction at the *Horten* workshop near Göttingen.

The entire nose wheel assembly on the *Ho 9 V2* as it appears on the final center section frame. The oleo shaft is vertical from its top down to the nose wheel fork unlike the oleo fork used on the *Ho 229 V3* which had been designed and built by one of *Gotha's* subcontractors.

A close up view of the Ho 9 V2's nose wheel showing the nose wheel fork and tire. The tire and rim itself was heavy...probably on the order of 150 pounds.

The Ho 9 V2's nose wheel assembly in the Ho 9 V2 under construction at the Horten workshop. A great deal of work has yet to be completed when this photograph was taken. The starboard side Jumo 004B is shown minus its air intake duct, starter motor, and circular starter motor fuel tank. It is not entirely clear if this is a brand new 004B here or an empty shell used only as a mock up while they waited for a ready-to-run 004B. If it were a ready-to-run 004B one would think that the engine would have been covered during construction of the center section in order to protect it from dust and dirt contaminating the compressor.

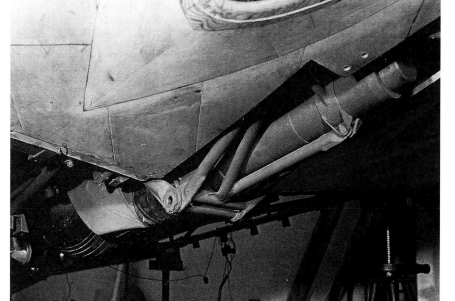

The Ho 9 V2 with the nose wheel fully retracted during construction of the center section frame. This author is unaware of photographs showing the nose wheel cover/doors and their full nature remains a mystery.

The main spar for the *Ho 9*. Shown is the wing root end of the all-wood main spar for the port outer wing being held steady by one of the *Horten Flugzeugbau* shop foremen.

This is how the *Ho 9 V2's* fully retracted undercarriage may have looked like. Digital image by *Mario Merino*.

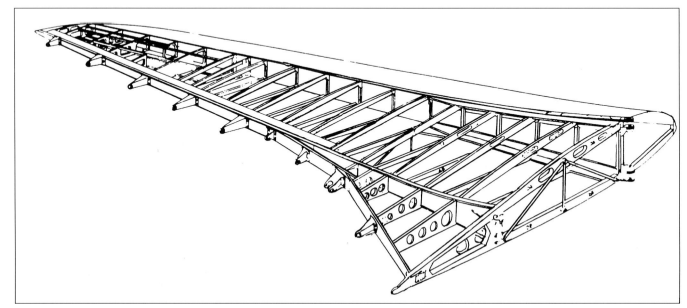

A pen and ink drawing by the *Horten Flugzeugbau* of the all-wood port outer wing internal arrangement for the *Ho 9 V1* sailplane.

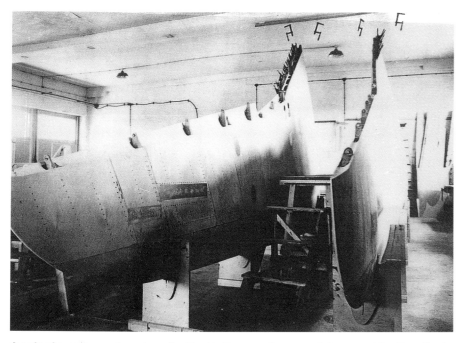

A pair of wooden outer wings for the *Ho 9* appearing complete except for the attachment of flight controls to the trailing edge. The two rectangular forms near the wing tip on the left-hand wing are the rudders.

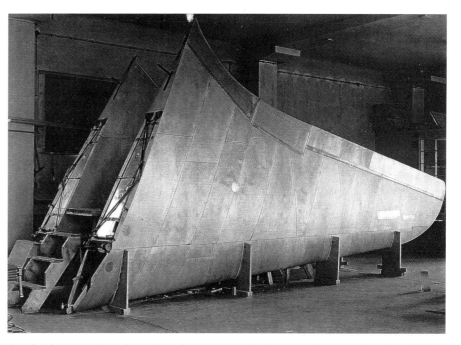

A pair of outer wings for a turbojet powered *Ho 9* complete except for joint filling, smoothing, and painting. The silver-appearing items in the wing root area are fuel tanks. It is not known if this pair of wings was for the *V2* or a spare set of fuel-carrying wings.

The *Ho 9 V2* at dawn with its twin *Jumo 004Bs* exhaust nozzles burning red hot as the all-wing begins its take-off role at Oranienburg. Digital image by *Mario Merino*.

The *Ho 9 V2* as seen from above and front showing the red-line step only boundaries. Digital image by *Mario Merino*.

An eye-level view of the *Ho 9 V2* on a snow-covered tarmac. Digital image by *Mario Merino*.

A nose on view of the one piece plexiglass cockpit windscreen on the *Ho 9 V2* and the twin *Jumo 004B's* close up showing their aluminum covered *Riedel* turbine starter motors. Digital image by *Mario Merino*.

The *Ho 9 V2* out on the snow covered tarmac shortly after being taken from its warm and dry hangar. Digital image by *Mario Merino*.

The modified *Ho 9 V2* with a vertical fin attached hinged rudder as seen from its front port side. Digital image by *Mario Merino*.

There was a lot of talk between critics and supporters alike regarding the need for a vertical fin with an attached rudder on the *Ho 9 V2*. *Walter* wanted to install a vertical fin/rudder on their *Ho 9 V2* and probably would have had *Reimar* do so if the *V2* had not been destroyed and the war lasted a few months longer. This is how the *Ho 9 V2* might have looked with a vertical fin/rudder. Digital image by *Mario Merino*.

The vertical fin/rudder version of the *Ho 9 V2* on a snow covered tarmac. Digital image by *Mario Merino*.

The nose gear cover appears like a "barn door" in this photo of the *Ho 9 V2* getting ready for a flight test at Oranienburg in January/February 1945.

The vertical fin/rudder version of the *Ho 9 V2* in powered flight out and about in mid 1945. Digital image by *Mario Merino*.

One of the more famous photos of the *Ho 9 V2* as seen at Oranienburg during its flight testing. The individual laying on the *V2's* starboard wing is *Jumo* jet engine expert who started the *004Bs* each time prior to take-off by *Horten* test pilot *Erwin Ziller*.

Horten test pilot *Erwin Ziller* looks out of the *V2's* cockpit right at the camera. This is one of the few photos we have of *Ziller* inside the *9 V2.*

One of the best views of the available of the *Ho 9 V2* and it shows how well *Reimar Horten* buried the *Jumo 004Bs* within the center section without creating bumps and bulges in the surface skin. Starboard side. Oranienburg January/February 1945.

A poor quality photo of the *Ho 9 V2* starting its take off run at Oranienburg January/February 1945. Notice the metal fender over the nose wheel.

One of the few photographs of the *Ho 9 V2* in flight. From this distance it is pretty difficult to tell if *Ziller* is taking off or landing the *V2*. Oranienburg January/February 1945.

This is the approximate location where *Erwin Ziller* and his *Ho 9 V2* crashed down on 18 February 1945 while attempting a landing at Oranienburg airfield. On the top of this embankment is a railroad track. Photo by the author in the early 1980s.

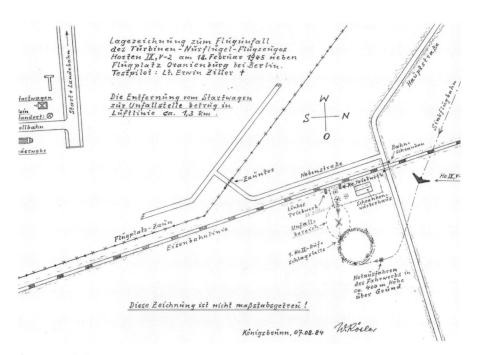

A extremely interesting map of the location where *Erwin Ziller* crashed down with his *Ho 9 V2* on 18 February 1945. This map was drawn by former *Horten* worker *Walter Rösler* from material provided by former *Horten* worker *Rudolf Preussler*. To the map's right can be seen the outline of the *Ho 9 V2* making its final approach to the Oranienburg airfield located in the upper left hand corner of the map. As the *V2* approaches it goes into a downward spiral and crashes perpendicular to the elevated railroad track. The exact position of the crash is a large red "X" and near the railroad gate keeper's house. Test pilot *Erwin Ziller* is propelled out of the *V2* into a fruit tree still strapped in his seat and falls to the snow-covered ground. He is dead when fellow *Horten* workers arrive at his side.

The crash down and wreckage field of the *Ho 9 V2*. Digital image by *Mario Merino*.

A view of the *V2* crash scene from the opposite side of railroad gate keeper's house. There was no fire. Digital image by *Mario Merino*.

A view of the *V2* crash scene from the railroad track. From this location we can see the path made by the twin *004Bs* took when they dismounted the center section frame both finally ending up at the base of the railroad track embankment. *Erwin Ziller* was found at the base of the fruit tree closest to the fence corner. Digital image by *Mario Merino*.

Top Right: The starboard side outer wing was pretty much destroyed in the crash leaving only its main spar still attached to the center section. *Erwin Ziller's* body still strapped in his seat was found at the base of the first fruit tree inside the railroad gate keeper's yard. Digital image by *Mario Merino*.

Right: The port side outer wing was intact having tore away from its attachment points to the center section frame. Fuel tanks inside the outer wings ruptured leaking jet fuel throughout the wreckage scene. Digital image by *Mario Merino*.

Erwin Ziller's funeral and burial in the City of Oranienburg. In the center of the photo is *Walter Horten*. A week later the *Horten* brothers would lose another of their test pilots *Hermann Strebel* in the crash of the laminar-flow *Ho 4B* sailplane.

Horten Flugzeugbau test pilot *Leutnant Erwin Ziller*.

The Horten Ho 229 V3

A *Ho 229* painted camouflage. It is armed with a pair of *MK 108* 30 mm cannon. Digital image by *Mario Merino*.

Above Left: A single color *Dark Green 83* painted *Ho 229* type *V3* with dawn breaking in the background. Digital image by Mario *Merino*.

Left: Red "*17*," a *Ho 229* in a banking turn showing its white painted underside. Digital image by *Mario Merino*.

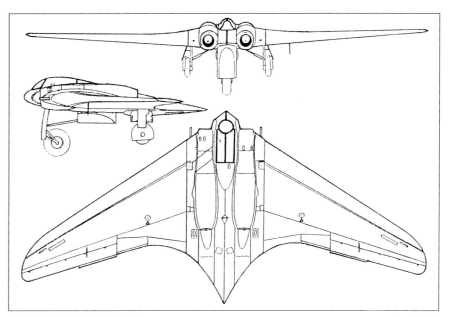

A pen and ink three-view general arrangement drawing of the *Ho 229 V3.*

The *Ho 229 V3* center section as found by American Army in early April 1945, Freidrichsroda with a bare center section frame behind probably the *V5* or *V6.* The *Gotha* workshop had been abandoned by its workers when the American troops arrived. Notice, too, the dirty nature of this workshop compared to the *Horten* workshop near Göttingen. This *V3* needed plywood covering to its port side and *General George McDonald*, director of Army Air Force Intelligence-Europe hired several former *Gotha* workers to complete the *V3's* center section.

The *Ho 229 V3* shortly after its arrival to Freeman Field late October 1945 from RAE-Farnborough, England. *Captain Eric Brown* wanted the *Ho 229 V3* for the RAE-Farnborough. *General George McDonald* gave him the all-wing machine and it was taken to England. Just exactly how it was transported is unknown at the present time. RAE wished to test fly the *V3* and before doing so wanted to equip the *V3* with *Rolls-Royce* "*Nene*" centrifugal turbojet engines. After a thorough evaluation by the RAE it was decided that replacing the axial flow *004Bs* with "*Nenes*" would require too much work and besides it was not clear if the test results would be worthwhile. The RAE shipped the *V3* to Freeman Field and it arrived in October 1945. The *V3* all-wing was never made flight ready.

The aft view of the *Ho 229 V3* when found by the Americans at Friedrichsroda in April 1945. This end of the *V3* appears complete except for covering aft the cockpit canopy.

Above Right: The *Ho 229 V3's* center section at Freeman Field, after its arrival from RAE- Farnborough, England about October 1945.

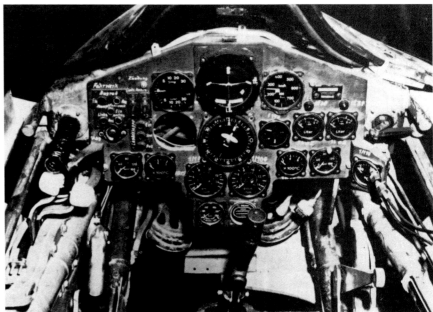

Right: The cockpit instrument panel of the *Ho 229 V3*. Freeman Field, about October 1945.

Rear port side view of the *Ho 229 V3's* center section. Freeman Field, about October 1945. This author is unaware of any photo of the *Ho 229 V3* with its outer wings attached.

The end view of the *Ho 229 V3's* center section at Freeman Field, about October 1945. The condition of the *V3's* aft portion looks pretty much the same as it did when it was first photographed at Friedrichsroda in April 1945.

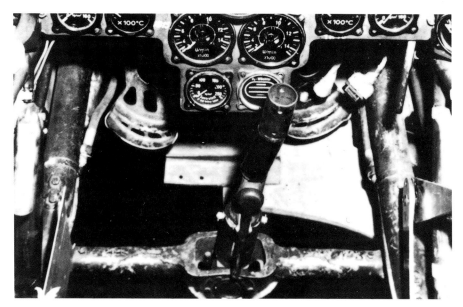

The control "stick" in the *Ho 229 V3.* Freeman Field, about October 1945.

The cockpit interior and instrument panel of the *Ho 229 V3* in storage at the National Air and Space Museum, Silver Hill, Maryland in the mid 1980s. Photograph by the author.

A starboard side nose view of the *Ho 229 V3's* center section in storage at the National Air and Space Museum, Silver Hill, Maryland. Photograph by the author in the mid 1980s.

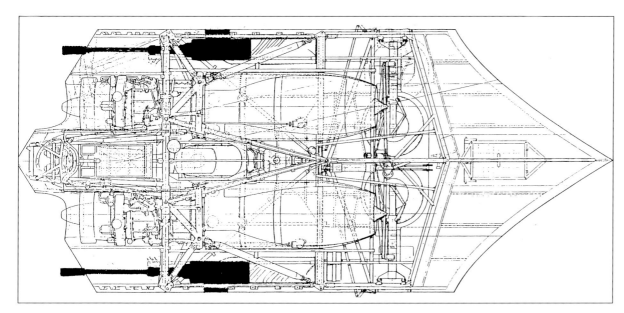

A pen and ink drawing of the *Ho 229* V3's *MK 108* 30 mm cannon installation in the center section. Illustration by *Arthur Bentley*.

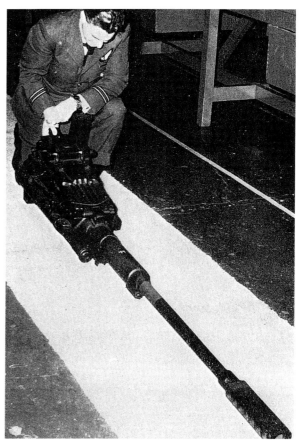

The *MK 108* 30 mm cannon of the type to be installed in the *Ho 229 V3* when it entered serial production for the Front. The British officer is noted aviation historian *Alfred Price*.

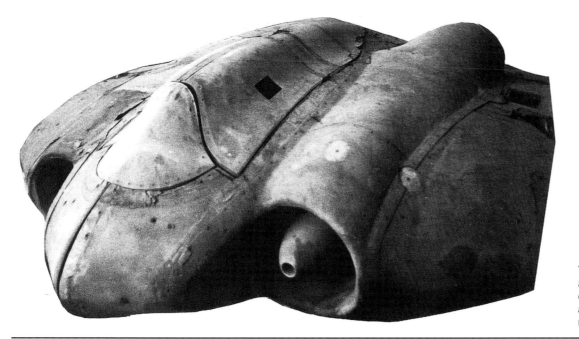

The only surviving *Ho 9* in the world...the *Ho 229 V3* in storage at the National Air and Space Museum, Silver Hill, Maryland. The current opaqueness of its cockpit canopy will be transparent again with a thorough cleaning. Photograph by the author in the mid 1980s.

The *Ho 229 V3* with its cockpit canopy pushed aft. Photograph by the author in the mid 1980s.

Below: The aft cockpit including pilot's seat of the *Ho 229 V3* in storage at the National Air and Space Museum, Silver Hill, Maryland in the mid 1980s. Photograph by the author.

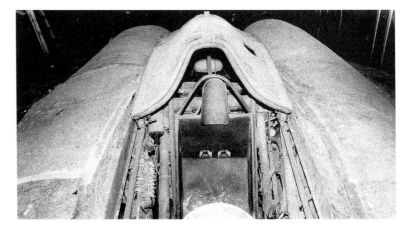

A starboard rear side view of the *Ho 229 V3.* Except for the deteriorated surface plywood and rusted tin aft the turbojet engines, the *V3* is in pretty good shape. Photograph by author in the mid 1980s.

The incomplete *Ho 229 V4* center section with *004B's* installed found also at *Gotha's* workshop in Friedrichsroda in April 1945. It appears that the *V4* was to be similar in lay out to the *V3*.

The *Ho 229 V3's* aft center section looking forward. The faint *Halkenkreuz* was painted on years ago in the United States. Serial production models in all likelihood would have had a *Halkenkreuz* in about the same location. The *Horten* brothers did not need a vertical surface to paint on the *Swastika*...most of their sailplanes carried the *Halkenkreuz* on flat surfaces.

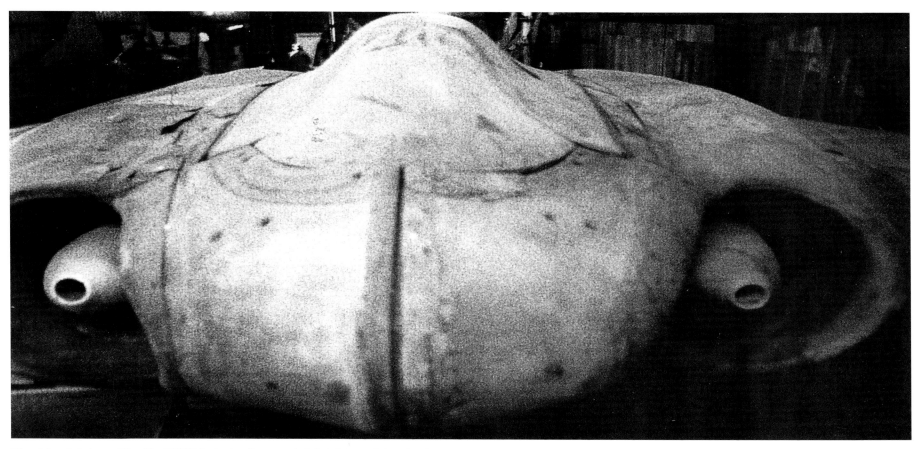

Direct frontal view of the *Ho 229 V3* featuring its round air intakes and the aluminum cones covering over its *Riedel* turbine starter motors. Photograph by the author in the mid 1980s.

A close up look at the *004B's* variable thrust control nozzle or "onion" as it is sometimes referred. The hot exhaust coming from the turbojet passed over tin to help prevent the plywood from catching on fire. Photograph by the author in the mid 1980s.

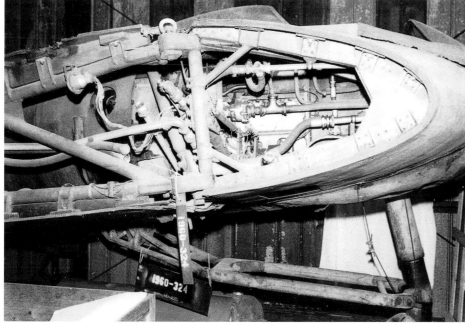

A close up look of the *Ho 229 V3* starboard center section. The starboard *Jumo 004B's* compressor section is visible. The round opening aft the compressor section is one of the several port holes where fuel was injected into the combustion chamber behind the opening. Photograph by the author in the mid 1980s.

An aft view of the *Ho 229 V4.* It appears that this center section was about ready for its plywood covering when *Gotha* workers abandoned their Friedrichsroda workshop in April 1945 as the American Army drew closer.

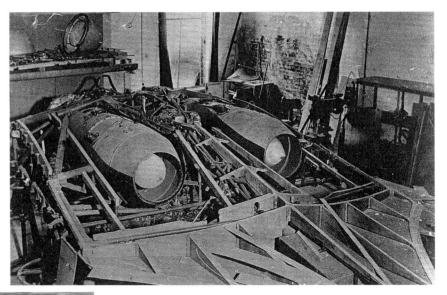

When *Ziller* died in the crash of the *Ho 9 V2* it eliminated any possibility of adding a vertical fin/rudder, though *Walter* wanted to add a vertical fin/rudder to the *V3* and test it with this configuration. How the *V3* would have looked with a vertical fin is unknown because there are no drawings known to this author of a tailed *Ho 9.* It is likely that the vertical finned *V3* would have looked similar to this impression. Digital image by *Mario Merino*.

A *V3* type *Ho 229* in flight carrying a vertical fin with an attached hinged rudder. Digital image by *Mario Merino*.

One of *Walter Horten's* wishes prior to war's end was to construct a vertical finned *Ho 229* like the one shown here on a snow covered tarmac. How would it have changed its directional stability...no change...better...and if so by how much? Digital image by *Mario Merino*.

What appears to be a complete welded up center section frame...perhaps the single seat *V5...found* also at *Gotha's* Friedrichsroda workshop. It is not known to this author just how many center section frames were found by the American Army at their Friedrichsroda workshop.

WEIGHTS, SPECIFICATIONS AND PERFORMANCE STATISTICS					
Aircraft type		Ho 229 V1	Ho 229 V2a	Ho 229 V2b	Ho 229 V3
Role		Test Prototype	Test Prototype	Test Prototype	Fighter Prototype
Seating		1	1	1	1
Wing Area	m² (ft²)	52 (560)	52 (560)	52 (560)	53 (570.5)
Wing Span	mm (ft-in)	16,760 (54 - 11¾)	16,760 (54 - 11¾)	16,760 (54 - 11¾)	16,800 (55 - 1⅜)
Length	mm (ft-in)	7,600 (24 - 11¼)	7,465 (24 - 6)	7,465 (24 - 6)	7,465 (24 - 6)
Height	mm (ft-in)			2,810 (9 - 2¾)	2,810 (9 - 2¾)
Weight Empty	kg (lb)	2,200 (4,850)	4,082 (9,000)	4,600 (10,140)	5,067 (11,170)
Takeoff Weight	kg (lb)	2,400 (5,291)	7,938 (17,600)	8,500 (18,739)	8,999 (19,840)
Engine type		None	2 x BMW 003 A-1	2 x Jumo 004 B-2	2 x Jumo 004 B-2
Maximum thrust	kg (lb)		798 (1,760)	900 (1,983)	900 (1,983)
Maximum speed at sea level	km/h (mph)			950 (590)	949 (590)
Maximum speed at 12 km (39,372 ft)	km/h (mph)		1,046 (650)	977 (607)	977 (607)
Cruise speed at 10 km (32,810 ft)	km/h (mph)		697 (433)	690 (429)	632 (393)
Service ceiling	km (ft)		15.8 (52,000)	16 (52,496)	15.8 (52,000)
Landing speed	km/h (mph)		145 (90)	145 (90)	156 (97)
Rate of climb	m/min (ft/min)		1,311 (4,301)	1,320 (4,331)	1,311 (4,301)
Flight duration	hrs		4.5	3.0	4.5
Armament		None	None	None	None

Courtesy: *David Myhra, Ho 229 Monogram Close-Up 12*, Monogram Aviation Publications, 1983.

A day fighting two man *Ho 229 V7* was proposed near war's end, too. The *V7* shown is with its *Jumo 004Bs* or *004Cs* burning bright and strong, is carrying a radar dish in its center section nose. Camouflage paint. Digital image by *Mario Merino*.

There are drawings from 1945 in existence from today of a proposed *Ho 229* two man day fighter and/or night fighter known as the *V7*. The *V7* design appears to have a double sweep back on the center section as shown in this *Horten Flugzeugbau* pen and ink illustration.

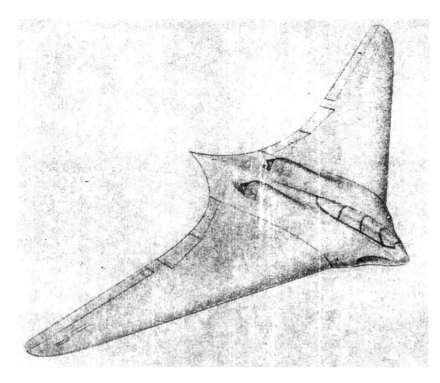

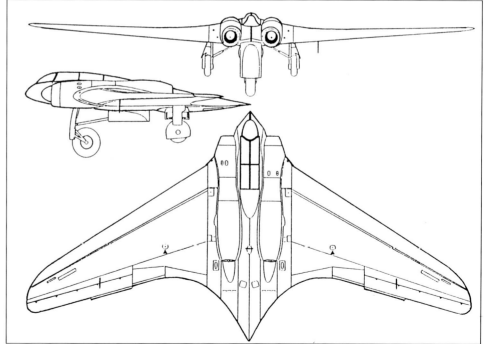

A pen and ink drawing of the proposed *Ho 229 V7* two man fighter. The nose gear cover shown is incorrect because research indicates that the nose wheel on the *V3*, at least, was a conventional two part hinged door to the fuselage.

The *Reimar Horten* modified *Ho 2B* sailplane featuring a double sweep back to the center section. This model was flown many times out of Göttingen to obtain data on the aerodynamics of a larger *Ho 9* with a double sweep back and a two man cockpit for day and/or night fighting.

A radar equipped two man *Ho 229 V7* night fighter in camouflage with a second machine behind and off to starboard. Digital image by *Mario Merino*.

A two man radar equipped *Ho 229 V7* night fighter in camouflage beginning its take off roll. Digital image by *Mario Merino*.

A overhead view of a two man radar equipped *Ho 229 V7* night fighter in camouflage on its take off roll. Digital image by *Mario Merino*.

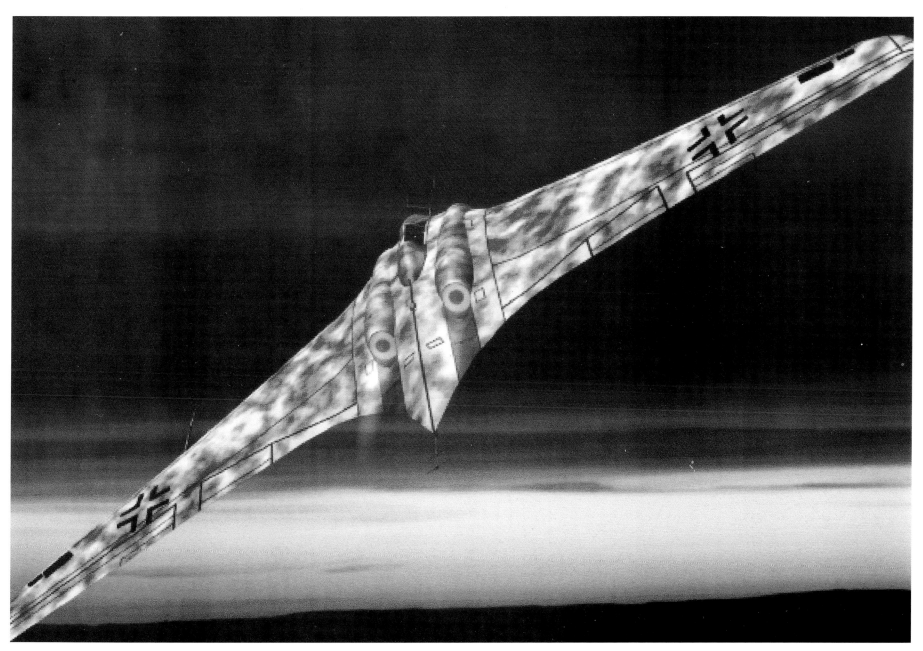

A "lone wolf" two man radar equipped *Ho 229 V7* night fighter at dawn shown in a banking turn off to port and home. Digital image by *Mario Merino*.

A *Ho 229 V7* at dawn and already out hunting for Allied bombers foolish enough to enter German airspace where this day fighter is on patrol duty today. Digital image by *Mario Merino*.

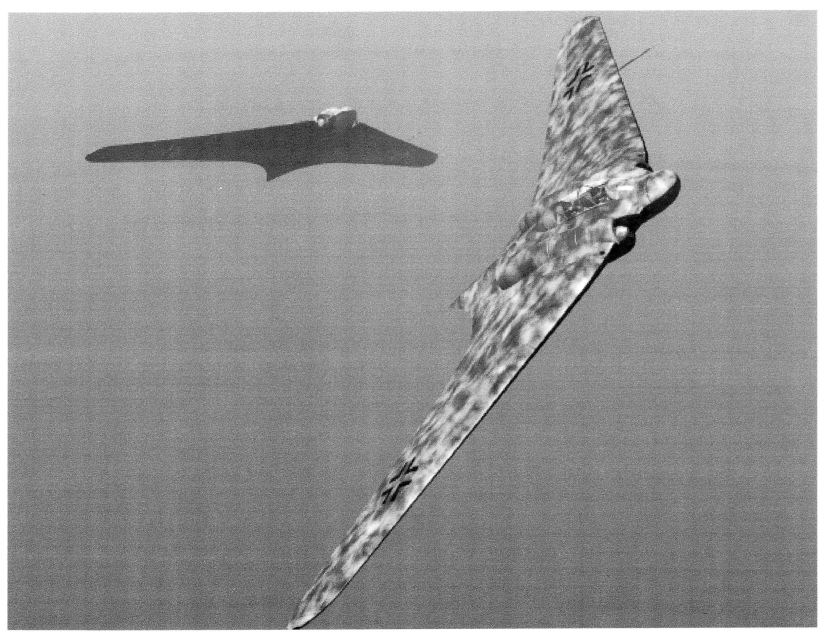

Looking like a *Klingon* "bird of prey," a second two man *Ho 229 V7* day fighter joins her sister ship at dawn and a "hunting" we shall go. Digital image by *Mario Merino*.

A two man *Ho 229 V7* day fighter is waiting on the tarmac at dawn for take off clearance. Digital image by *Mario Merino*.

A pair of two man radar equipped *Ho 229 V7's* night fighters roaming German skies in search of Allied night bomber formations. In the foreground is "*Red 11*" painted in black while a sister ship flying off to port is painted in camouflage. Digital image by *Mario Merino*.